ON COURT QUICK-FIX BOOKLET

TENNIS STRATEGY

HOW TO BEAT ANY STYLE PLAYER

Grant Grinnell—Tennis Professional

www.grantgrinnelltennis.com

QUICK-FIX BOOKS BY GRANT GRINNELL

Tennis Strategy: How to Beat Any Style Player

ISBN-13: 978-1514729717
ISBN-10: 1514729717

BISAC: Sports & Recreation | General

Printed by CreateSpace
Available from www.createspace.com/5585101

INTRODUCTION

Beat any style of player

This 1-2-3 book gives you tactics to beat any style of player, singles or doubles. The tips are pointed, cut right to the chase, are in layman's terms and can be implemented to empower you at will. The goal of the book is to give you an A-B-C game plan tailored to your unique style and skills.

The book is divided into four sections. The first section will teach you different styles of play, how to analyze your opponent and how to handle important match play moments.

The second two sections focus on how to adapt your game and problem solve to beat any style of opponent in singles or doubles.

The fourth section provides quick-fix mental toughness tools to free your mind and emotions from blocking the natural flow of your body.

About the author

Grant Grinnell is a certified instructor with 35 years of coaching experience—over 50,000 hours of on-court coaching. He has dedicated his entire career to helping students find their best fast.

Grant has carefully created this book considering your precious time, your ability to understand the content and fearlessly apply it to your game. Please feel free to contact Grant at www.wholelifetennis.com or purchase the app version of his book at tennisstrategy123.com.

How to use the book

First find a highlighter, start in the mental toughness section and then go through the entire book highlighting every word, phrase or sentence that resonates with you in a way you can apply to your game. Then use the tactics to adapt your game to the style of your opponents to defeat them.

If you don't have the necessary skills, take the strategy book to your coach and communicate the tactic you would like to develop. Coaches should use the book as a resource for lesson plans based on the ability level and natural affinity of your students. Help them develop an A, B, C plan for their unique match play style.

CONTENTS

UNDERSTANDING YOUR STYLE AND YOUR OPPONENT'S

Styles of match play

1. Pusher-consistent baseliner: This style of player loves to keep the ball in play at all costs to wear down their opponents with their relentless consistency.
2. Aggressive baseliner: This style of player has reached a level of consistency and has developed a big weapon in the form of a big forehand or backhand groundstroke.
3. One volley finisher: This style of player uses great groundstrokes to put his opponents on defense, and then moves into the net for easy one volley finishes.
4. Net rusher: This style of player prefers the volley and attacks the net at their earliest opportunity to exert pressure and finish the point quickly.
5. All-court players: This style of player is just as proficient from the baseline as the net. They have achieved a degree of mastery from all areas of the court.

How I analyze my opponent

1. Does your opponent prefer a high or low ground stroke at contact point? Give them the opposite of their preferred strike zone.
2. Is your opponent slow of foot side-to-side or moving up or back? Challenge their weakness.

3. Does your opponent prefer the backcourt or the net? Whatever their preferences, force them to play in an area of the court they're less comfortable in.
4. Does your opponent have a weaker forehand or backhand? Exploit their weakness.
5. Does your opponent prefer a fast- or slow-paced shot? Mix speeds to keep them out of rhythm.
6. Does your opponent handle pressure well? Look for your opponent to crack mentally or emotionally and stretch the lead by capitalizing on their lack of focus.

Important match play moments

1. Pre-match: Visualize yourself warming up well, analyzing your opponent, getting the early lead, playing well under pressure, handling adversity, and closing out the match. By doing so you will be able to translate your visualizations to the current match as if you've already been there.
2. Pre-match warm-up: Find a court to warm up on prior to your match.
3. Match play warm-up: Focus entirely on timing and rhythm, build up to your normal pace, and analyze your opponent.
4. The first few games: Percentages say get an early lead and you'll win the first set. Increase your margin of error on strokes, build up to your normal pace and keep analyzing your opponent.
5. Create a game plan maximizing your strengths while exploiting your opponent's weaknesses.

6. Maintaining the lead: Once you break serve, have the mindset that the next game is the most important game of the match.
7. Momentum switches: Go back to your game plan if the momentum switches against you.
8. Closing out your opponent: Keep applying the pressure that got you there and expect your opponent's best tennis.

HOW TO BEAT ANY STYLE: SINGLES PLAYERS

How to beat a big server

This opponent creates havoc with this decisive weapon, either ending the point or setting up an easy winner on the next shot.

1. Watch the server's toss closely to anticipate the spin, pace, and placement of the serve.
2. Stand up or back to position your body to return waist high.
3. Stand back to give yourself more reaction time.
4. Split step when you see the server's racket come up from behind their back.
5. Take your racket back by turning your shoulders and start your backswing directly behind the ball. Avoid a quick arm motion.
6. Track the ball longer and focus on the contact point later just prior to the ball hitting the strings.
7. Block the ball using a six to eighteen inch follow through.
8. Target high returns to weakness or deep down the middle.
9. Slice to buy more reaction time off the return.
10. Place the return so you can play your strength on the next shot.
11. Attack the second serve and transfer pressure back on the server.

How to beat a great returner

This opponent transfers pressure right back on the server with a deep or well-placed return that forces a weak response from the server.

1. Adjust your serving position on the baseline if necessary to serve to their weaker side.
2. Serve high spin or wide slice to keep the ball out of their strike zone.
3. Experiment and place the serve in an area of the service box where your opponent is forced to play to your strength on the next shot.
4. Reduce your serve speed by 20% to increase first-serve percentage.
5. Serve and volley to keep returner out of rhythm.
6. Serve wide to open up the court to attack their weakness.
7. Serve into the body so they can't load their weight behind the shot.
8. Serve down the middle so they can't create angles off the return.
9. Vary your spin, speed and placement to keep the returner out of rhythm.

How to beat an all-court player

The all-court player is just as solid from the baseline as the net. Sometimes they lack a big weapon but they make up for it with a variety of tools in their bag. Although they can play from anywhere in the court, they will still have some areas of weakness and can be exploited.

1. Be prepared for your opponent to change tactics quickly.
2. Use your weapon to dictate as much as possible.
3. Serve and return to a location to play your strength on the next shot.
4. Hit moon balls to offset the volley portion of their game. Keep this player off balance rhythmically.
5. Find the weakness. Adapt and automate your style as necessary.
6. Mix speed, spin and height of your shots to keep opponent out of rhythm.
7. Increase your first-serve percentage so your opponent can't attack a weak second serve.
8. Take the ball on the rise to limit opponent's reaction time.
9. Keep the ball out of their favorite strike zone by slicing.
10. Use excessive topspin when they come to the net.

How to beat an aggressive baseliner

The aggressive baseliner does not have the personality or style to grind it out and prefers to attack early in points with a big forehand or backhand.

1. Hit high and deep moon balls to force them further back behind the baseline. Don't allow this player to control the tempo of points with their big weapon.
2. Slice low to keep the ball out of their power zone.
3. Approach down the center of the court so you're not giving them the angle or a target.

4. Keep your opponent on the move so they can't load and explode on the ball.
5. Don't be surprised if they hit a lot of winners or try to rush you through the match.
6. Finesse low volleys to make passing shots more difficult.
7. Take the ball on the rise to give them less time to set up.
8. Draw or drop shot your opponent to the net and lob or pass them.
9. Serve into the body on either side so opponent can't load their weight into the shot.
10. Be light on your feet and be a retriever so you can bait them into over-hitting. Make them play one more ball!

How to beat a serve-and-volleyer - net rusher

The net rusher is a player who likes to attack the net early and often. Their volleys are usually much stronger than their groundstrokes and they don't have the patience to grind out long points. They usually move better up and back rather than side-to-side.

1. Serve and return or approach and volley to take the net away from this opponent.
2. Return cross-court because you have more court to hit to.
3. Hit moon balls to pin your opponent well behind the baseline.
4. Hit excessive topspin on return of serve or passing shots to keep the ball down.

5. Chip soft returns or passing shots to keep the ball down at their feet.

6. Use offensive lobs early to open up passing lanes, topspin lobs if they close the net, or over their backhand side if the opportunity presents.

7. Hit the ball on the rise to take away opponent's time.

8. Hit the inside or the outside of the ball to create angles on passing shots.

9. Increase first-serve percentage so they can't attack your second serve and move into the net.

10. Place your serve wide to stretch opponent and get them moving away from the net.

11. Serve into their body to get opponent to step back to deter a straight shot to the net.

How to beat a pusher or counter-puncher

The pusher/counterpuncher is a baseline backboard and moon baller who loves to win by grinding it out, running everything down, using your pace against you and keeping the ball in play at all costs.

1. Slice wide or use drop shots on your return of serve to pull pusher off the baseline.

2. Use drop shots during rallies to pull your opponent off the baseline and pass or lob.

3. Make the pusher play from no man's land by drawing them in and then hitting around them as they retreat to the baseline.

4. Go the net and use angle or finesse volleys to open up the court and move them off the baseline.

5. Hit to the center of the court on approach shots so they have less chance of creating angles.
6. Hit moon balls then angle to keep them off the baseline.
7. Hit behind opponent as they recover to offset their quickness.
8. Move the pusher into defensive position, sneak into the net and volley to open court.
9. Don't give the pusher hard shots; let them create their own pace.
10. Don't get discouraged and try to hit winners or rush to finish points.
11. In general, don't let the pusher push.

How to beat a hacker-slicer

This player slices everything and usually has a very unorthodox style. Your ability to finish points is paramount against this type of player.

1. Prepare for an ugly battle and do not lose your cool.
2. Go to the net because their shots tend to float a little more.
3. Move a little closer to where the ball is bouncing to set up.
4. Keep your feet moving to make any sudden last second adjustments.
5. Expect the ball to stay low, so bend lower than usual.
6. Drop your seat and waist to the height of the low slice and stay down throughout the shot.
7. Serve and volley to take advantage of any floaters.
8. Don't give this player any power to use against you.

9. Hit high moon balls to their weaker side to force your opponent back and keep the ball out of their strike zone.

How to beat the soft or weak server

This type of player has a very soft serve that lures opponents into over hitting or playing the ball out of their strike zone.

1. Use more excessive topspin on the return.
2. Stand in a position to play your strength off the return.
3. Play the ball in your strike zone around waist high.
4. Play a drop shot off the return as a safe alternative.
5. Slice the ball wide off the return.
6. Pay extra attention to your footwork so you don't get sluggish.
7. Match the same speed of the serve if you find yourself over-hitting.
8. Keep your composure if you miss the shot. Project a strong image as if to say "no problem." Keep a positive inner voice.

SECTION 3:
HOW TO BEAT ANY STYLE: DOUBLES TEAMS

How to beat big-serving teams

1. Watch the ball-toss placement to anticipate direction, spin and speed of the serve.
2. Court-position up or back to hit the return of serve waist-high in your strike zone. Always return around waist height.
3. Shoulder-turn your backswing directly behind the contact point and focus on an extended follow through. Avoid a quick arm motion.
4. Focus on making contact on the inside or outside of the ball to create angle away from the net person.
5. Block the return and control court position by getting to the net.
6. Stand on the server's strength and make them serve to the other side of the service box.
7. Lob the return of serve to buy time.
8. Play two back on the baseline so there is no net person to attack off the return.

How to beat great returning teams

1. Adjust your serving position on the baseline to serve to their weaker side.
2. Play Australian formation to take away the cross court return.
3. Serve wide slice or high spin out of their strike zone.

4. Lob to buy time after the return of your serve.
5. Angle your serve to elicit a weaker response and create holes to target.
6. Serve into the body so they can't load their weight behind the shot.
7. The server's partner should create a balance of activity at the net by poaching, faking and playing formations to distract the returner and force them to think and to take secondary shots.
8. Position both players on the baseline to buy more time and wait for a more offensive opportunity.

How to beat teams that control the net

1. Serve into the body to slow the progress of the net rusher.
2. Focus your target on a point and height over the net and not an area in the court. This will help keep the ball low and out of your opponents strike zone.
3. Use more excessive topspin when your opponents are at the net.
4. Bounce the ball in front of or behind your opponent so they are forced to hit up.
5. Lob off the return to force them away from the net.
6. Use the topspin lob if either opponent closes just prior to your final preparation. Lob over their backhand side as a preference.
7. Chip a wide-angle return inside your opponent's service line.
8. Take the return of serve earlier to reduce their reaction time.

9. Position both players on the baseline to buy time and draw out points. Try to make it a dog day for this type of opponent.

How to beat one-up one-back teams

1. Make an extra effort to play the ball a little more cross court to take away the net player.
2. Draw the baseliner into the net and keep the volleyer pinned to the baseline.
3. Play lobs off the returns to keep the strong volleyer pinned back on the baseline.
4. Try to make your opponents take at least 3 steps to make contact with each shot.
5. Hit short angle or finesse volleys to draw the strong baseline player into the net.
6. Play all finishing overheads and chest-high volleys to the player closest to the net or down the middle. Angle overheads to create space to target.
7. Control low volleys to the deep player.
8. Play Australian formation when serving to take away a strong return of serve that's in rhythm.
9. Serve wide to create holes to target between your opponents.

How to beat lobbing teams

1. Communicate with your partner to avoid wasted movement and increase your reaction time as a team.
2. From the baseline, move diagonally foreword and take lobs out of the air to decrease your opponent's reaction time.

3. Use angle overheads to finish a point or to open up the court.
4. Hit overheads like overheads and high volleys like high volleys.
5. Finesse or angle volleys to give opponent less court to lob to.
6. Stand back slightly at the net when your partner is serving.
7. Slice and draw your opponent into the net with your return of serve.
8. Play one player a little closer to the net and the other a little further back, to protect the lob.
9. Play Australian formation to put the net person's overhead in the center of the court.
10. Position both players on the baseline, pick the weaker player and make it a dog day for them.

How to beat poaching teams

1. Watch the server's toss location and movement after the serve to pick up any cues on the poacher movement.
2. Return at the net person early in the match to send a message to limit their movement.
3. Play with more excessive topspin to keep the ball down.
4. Lob the return to take away poach.
5. Don't change your mind mid-stroke. Pick your target and hit it.
6. Hit returns on the rise to decrease the net person's reaction time.
7. Slice shot angles wide out of the range of the poacher.

8. Position both players on the baseline to negate the poacher.

How to beat a team with one hot player

1. Communicate with your partner to develop a game plan.

2. Isolate the weaker player's side-to-side or up-back movement.

3. Make the weaker player feel like it's two players on one, playing and attacking them exclusively.

4. Lob your return over the stronger player's head and attack the weaker player.

5. Serve, return and approach with stronger angles on the weaker player to open up court.

6. When serving, play Australian formation on the weaker player's side and target your shots to the singles sideline. This will keep the ball out of the stronger players range.

7. Force the stronger and weaker player to play in their least favorite areas of the court, baseline or net.

8. Only play the hot player when finishing shots.

9. Play two-back if the strong player is dominating on serve, return of serve or poach.

10. Frustrate the stronger player by limiting their play and make it a dog day for the weaker player by frustrating them.

MENTAL QUICK-FIXES

Winning and losing

Attitudes regarding winning and losing probably cause more stress and frustration than any other mental component in sports. Simply stated, winning is IMPROVING.

This performance-based philosophy should be applied to both practice and competitive play. The true definition of winning is to IMPROVE your style, not to win the competition. Playing your style means playing the strength of your game plus taking an incremental step to improve your game on that day!

Example 1: your style/the strength of your game is to be a consistent baseliner who would like to play more aggressive shots on short balls. The incremental step for the day would be to try to hit more winners off short balls.

Example 2: your style is to be an aggressive baseliner who would like to put your opponent on defense, sneak up into the court and put the volley away. The incremental step would be to try to play more points at the net.

Example 3: your style is an all-court player who is extremely versatile and loves to exploit opponents. Your opponent is an aggressive baseliner with a big forehand. The incremental step would be to make a tactical adjustment of hitting moon balls to keep the ball out your opponent's strike zone.

In all these cases a win is not defined by winning the match but by playing the strength of your game and taking the incremental step to improve from the beginning to the end of the match. Any mental, technical, or tactical adjustment counts as an incremental step if you so choose. The end game is to keep taking the incremental step with as little thought as possible until your successes have become automated.

The advantages of taking the incremental improvement as a win are:

1. You will have more fun because you'll experience a greater sense of control relating to your technique, tactics, adjustments, and whatever you're working on. You're free to win and free to lose, yet free to improve and play up to your ability! Simply stated it's a more achievable and fulfilling long-term goal.

2. You will play with less pressure because you're focused in the moment on the incremental step, not on winning and losing. Your opponent's thinking, "What if I lose?" while you're thinking, "Improve my style." In other words, your mind and emotion won't block the natural flow of your body because you are not obsessed with the win or loss.

3. You will improve faster because you're taking the ego out of it and continually refining your game to the next level, rather than falling back into the same old patterns. With this philosophy, you will evolve rather than revolve. This is why pros look so surprised when they get the biggest wins of their lives. Their style has finally caught up to them, one incremental success built upon another!

Let's review the fine points one more time just to make sure we have it. Your style is your strength plus the incremental step you're taking to improve. The incremental step may also be in the form of any tactical, mental or emotional adjustment. You decide!

To play your style successfully, commit to letting go of your ego and compete for your potential rather than the win. Eventually you will improve to the point where winning and losing are just a function of your style and incremental successes. The true definition of winning is improving and improving is simply taking an incremental step that day. There is no such thing as a loss, either you win or improve.

My competition

The right attitude regarding competition is: I am my own competition and my goal is to play to the upper limits of my ability. Predetermined thoughts such as "I am expected to win" or "I am expected to lose" create a comparative mind trap that can backfire in competition. If you focus on the loss or the victory instead of your style, your mind and emotions may block the natural flow of your body and inhibit your performance.

The pros focus on transformation, not on the loss or the gain, and so should club-players. The key to transformation is to focus on developing your potential with as little thought of loss or gain as possible. Take the incremental step!

This doesn't mean that you're not interested in the style and tendencies of your opponent. You are. Your instincts are an invaluable tool! You may want to scout your opponent and exploit their weaknesses. The challenge is not to personalize them into a win-loss mindset that could block your ability to flow in the moment. To summarize, not understanding that you are your own competition leads to irrelevant thinking, choking, and "good day – bad day" performances.

If you have the right attitude about competition, you will be more interested in improving your style and you won't allow the expectation of the win or loss of the match to break the flow of your game.

All you can ask is to stretch the upper limits of your ability on a given day. Meaning play your style and take the incremental step as your philosophy of what winning is. Your competition is simply there as an expression of your personal style, talent and versatility. In the end it all comes back to you, the fire/effort, and the mindsets you've chosen self-liberate yourself in the fear free moment!

Coping with the philosophy transition

What? Winning isn't winning? I'm my own competition? Yes! Here are the stages you will go through as you make your amazing transformation. First you'll need to buy in and resolutely believe that winning is improving, and improving is taking the incremental step.

Plus, you must accept the fact that you are your own competition, and your only competition is with yourself to improve. You must resolutely believe that transformation is the end game and have an insatiable desire to come off the court a better player, even if you lose the match. You must improve at narrowing your focus, finding the good, and not moving on until you have achieved incremental mastery.

This is why I prepared the evaluation sheet at the end of the book for you so you can measure your incremental successes, build one on top of the other, and move from an outcome based must win philosophy to the performance based philosophy of take the incremental step. As you fill out the form and self-rate over time, you will find your focus beginning to change, and you will shimmy between the feelings of wanting to win and a newfound determination to come off the court a better player. At some point you'll realize you have been trying to manage so many misplaced attitudes and see the incremental step as something more achievable, something you can control, and something that will bring a greater measure of satisfaction, regardless of the outcome of the match.

As the process continues, you'll begin to see your incremental focus has improved your game, you're playing with less pressure, and you're having more fun. You'll enjoy different seasons of taking the improvement as the win, balancing improving with winning, and just enjoying your new plateaus. At the final stage, your expression will be more beautiful to you; you will be able to put your ego aside and play for the sheer joy of the game. You'll realize that your mental approach has changed your experience with the game—free to win and free to lose, yet free to play up to and stretch the upper limits of your ability.

The mental, emotional and physical connection

The next two headings, the mental, physical and emotional connection, moving your physiology, and adversity are insights from highly respected Dr. Jim Loehr. I recommend his "Mental Toughness Training for Sports" books for a more comprehensive perspective.[1] He is simply brilliant!

During competition, it's important to know where you want to be mentally, emotionally and physically so you can control your intensity levels. For example, mentally you may want to be calm, not frantic; emotionally you want to be nonjudgmental, less critical of your mistakes; physically you may want relaxed intensity. Each one of these areas is like a radar frequency you're gauging and automating throughout your competitions.

For example, if you mentally have poor self-talk during competition, emotionally you may become frustrated, physically your heart begins to race and your muscles tighten. Or, if you're physically to tired, you may mentally start to tell yourself you don't have what it takes to compete and then emotionally lose your fire. Or perhaps, if you're emotionally too self-judgmental, your performance suffers under pressure out of fear, then physically you play too fast while mentally you ask yourself, "Why me?" The key point here is if one area is off, then all areas are off!

All these mental, emotional, and physical states have an intensity level unique to the individual. Some play too high physically; some suffer from nerves; others think too much. All these connections must be self-regulated to create balance, rhythm and trust. It's difficult to control what you're not aware of, so understanding and becoming more intimately aware of the correlations among your mental,

---

[1] Loehr, James E. *Mental Toughness Training for Sports: Achieving Athletic Excellence.* New York: New American Library, 1986.

emotional and physical states is paramount to your attaining competitive balance and a level peak performance state.

Moving your physiology

One of the first steps toward freedom on the court is to acknowledge that you have a choice in how you will respond and take responsibility for your performance state of being (i.e., your mental, emotional, physical state).

The key is moving your emotions towards what you want, not what you don't want. By more disciplined thinking, visualizing and feeling, you will create a bio - chemical reaction in your body and move your physiology toward your best performance day. This is the difference between good and world-class competitors. The greats have the ability to move their self-image and their inner physiology from fear to poise, pressure to assurance, anxiety to calmness, frustration to resiliency, and losses to wins.

Make it your style to create and recreate positive emotional states at will, especially when you're not feeling them in the moment. This is a great life lesson and the difference between a great and very average performance!

Automated match play

Peak match play performances may take the form of playing the strength of your game with less technical focus as you find a way to exploit your opponent strategically. The incremental step (winning) would be to play as automated as possible as relates to your tactical, mental and emotional style.

Simply stated, over-thinking causes your strokes and movement patterns to break down. What was once automatic is now performed through too much conscious thought, which inhibits your ability to flow.

There are times or seasons when you will want to enjoy your new plateaus with as little thought as possible. This is completely expectable and essential and can culminate in a beautiful competitive season and/or self-expression.

Bottom line, there is always going to be an incremental step in the form of a mental, technical, or strategic adjustment during match play. Your peak performance goal under these circumstances is to become so automated even your adjustments are automated. As you evolve you will enjoy longer gaps of no-mind or auto-adaptive magical unconscious competency.

Adversity

All of us must be trained to handle adversity during competition, and the key is to respond and not react. Preparing my students that adversity in sports competitions is more likely to happen than not is an essential part of their training. Examples of adversity include encountering poor sportsmanship, cheating, anger, unauthorized involvement, referee errors, pettiness, and disappointments.

An athlete surprised or startled by adversity will not be able to play up to their ability and the recovery time could cost them the competition. The best plan is to call your opponent/s to the net and calmly discuss the concern. Always pre-plan a mindset for how you will handle uncomfortable situations so you can have more fun!

Flip the script on your mental toughness wall

A mental toughness wall would be a way of thinking on court that disempowers you during competition. For example, your judgmental thinking is affecting your nerves and making you consistently perform poorly.

1. Have a spiritual or universal perspective overall and remember it's just a game!
2. Determine what your primary mental wall or issues are. For example, winning and losing, nerves, pressure, fear, mistakes, competition, choking or anything disempowering your performance.
3. Determine how your current thinking, visualizations or emotions are disempowering you.
4. Write down the disempowering script you are currently following in as much detail as possible.
5. Now, write a new script with more disciplined thinking, feelings, and visualizations that will empower you and move you toward your best performance day.
6. Follow the new script in practice and competitive play.
7. Expect a shimmy between the old and the new, spiraling upward toward the new script as you feel more empowered.
8. Remember mental toughness is a process driven rather than result oriented approach. Facing and conquering inner obstacles translates into external successes. Take the initiative!

Improving

Use the pre and post match evaluation sheet at the end of the book and clearly define your incremental match play steps. Rate yourself on your performance, adjustments, what you did well and what you need to improve on in the future.

The pre/post evaluation sheet envelops you in process mode and eases you away from outcome mode. Written analysis of your matches simply improves focus and puts you on the fast track to improving your game. My students who take ten minutes to commit to this process spiral up at a much faster rate.

1. Focus on playing your game/style and not winning and losing.
2. Understand you are your own competition and the goal is to incrementally stretch the upper limits of your ability.
3. Make it your holy grail to take the incremental step technically, mentally, or strategically as your primary focus. Enjoy the plateau but crave the breakthrough.
4. Believe transformation is the end game, not winning and losing, so your mind and emotion won't block the natural flow of your body.
5. Resolutely believe in your style, your unique game! This will build confidence, motivation, and commitment for future progress.
6. You have a four times greater chance of improving if you "Tai-Chi" (shadow drill) your strokes in super slow motion. Three single acts of perfection twice a day.
7. It takes 300-500 repetitions to develop a new stroke. Without Tai-Chi, students typically have to go through a relearning process because things are still happening

to fast in practice secessions. The brain needs more time to engrave the full motor skill and relearning a missed step can take hundreds of more repetitions. As a coach with over 50,000 hours on the court, at times I'd rather see my students do ten minutes of slow motion shadow drilling to fix a long-term flaw than an hour and a half of on-court play.

8. Take the mental game seriously and have a proactive rather than a reactive approach for every competitive situation.

9. There is no such thing as a loss. Whether you win or improve, it's a victory.

Handling nerves

1. Reframe nerves as "everyone has them, and they are a launching pad to my game today." Smile.

2. Think of your nerves as beneficial because whatever is bringing them on means something deeply to you, as an expression of yourself.

3. Prepare a script with more disciplined thinking, imaging and feeling for your nerves. Embrace the proactive process prior to your matches.

4. Focus on moving your inner physiology toward your best performance day, as needed.

5. Visualize your best performance moment just prior to tensions moment. Create those invincible feelings.

6. Keep your eyes present, positive and relevant to the moment. Your eyes should be on your opponent, the ball, or your strings so your mind won't visually wonder off the court to irrelevant thoughts such as

who's watching the match, or activity surrounding the court.

7. Go into your breathing and release the tension.
8. Take an inventory of your body and release muscle tension.
9. Over time, take all the above and automate it as unconscious rituals.
10. Remember "no stress, no growth; no growth, no stress." Embrace the journey.

Pressure

1. Focus on playing your style, not the win or loss.
2. The incremental step here is to stay automated and not be too reliant on conscious thought. Use the technical and tactical rhythms you have already engraved.
3. Don't do anything brilliant, stupid or out of character. Play the ball and the strategy more than the score. Be at your best when it counts most.
4. Love the battle, be challenged not threatened by the situation.
5. A situation can't feel pressure only a person can. Take responsibility for your inner peak performance state.
6. Keep a strong positive image regardless of what you're feeling inside.
7. Recreate feelings, pictures and trigger words of incredibly successful moments under pressure, just prior to the pressure filled moment.
8. Use these pictures, words and feeling to empower you!

9. Use the mantras such as "I love the pressure and I'm really going to enjoy this moment." Then put it on autopilot with those feelings and sense of knowing.

10. Learn to love what you hate about your mental game. Think of it as developing a new fresh/ clear inner voice.

11. Do not over think strokes or tactics. Too much conscious thought blocks rhythm, flow and trust. Keep a positive inner voice.

12. Remember choking is a bio-chemical event.

13. Do not change the pacing of match or competition. Keep the same tempo if possible. Taking too much time between points causes choking.

14. Your zone means playing completely self - liberated, free from fear, flowing in the instinctive moment. Completely automated.

15. Obi-Wan Kenobi might say "don't want, don't think, just do!"

Mistakes

1. Universally understand growth is impossible without mistakes and learn and adapt from them.

2. Don't get overwhelmed, keep a positive inner voice. Make the adjustment, take the incremental step.

3. Negative thoughts create mental and physical dissent that hinders performance. A positive mind is a successful mind.

4. See if you can find the good in your error whether in strategy or execution.

5. Use the mantras "next time" or "good error" and move on.
6. Visualize the desired outcome or shadow drill the proper adjustment.
7. Remember that every thought, picture and feeling is creating a chemical reaction in your body.
8. Re-center your physiology in an empowering direction for optimal mental, emotional, and physical balance.
9. Great athletes are great actors so project a confident image and persona. Smile!
10. Automate your game and adapt to your mistakes as necessary.
11. Think to yourself "my style is so automated, even my adaptions have become automated."
12. If you feel anxiety, use it as a trigger to change your style/game to a more productive tactic.
13. There is no such thing as a loss, you either win or improve.

Choking

1. The key is to realize that everyone chokes and to develop your coping skills.
2. Limit your thoughts as much as possible and flow in the stroke and movement rhythmus/ patterns you have already ingrained. Too much thought creates hitches in stroke rhythms and movement patterns.
3. Remember your feelings during a moment in a prior competition when you competed unbelievably successfully then visualize and re-create those feeling

inside you just prior to the current competitive moment.

4. Control your eyes and what you're looking at, so you can control your thoughts. There is a direct relationship between what you look at and what you think. Don't bring any irrelevant thoughts into your mind which may inhibit your performance. Keep your eyes on your opponent, your strings or the ball.

5. Play your style, free to win and free to lose, yet free to play up to your ability. Keep all mental, emotional, and physical rhythms as automated as possible.

6. Breathe and feel the relaxed intensity as you re-center.

7. If any negativity comes into your mind, don't attach to a runaway train. This means let any negative thoughts pass right through you without attaching them, and creating a bio-chemical event in your body which could derail your style.

8. Stay in time tempo, excessive thinking or time lapses lead to choking.

9. Keep a positive self-image and inner voice regardless of the outcome. Embrace and love the battle.

10. Remember the mental, emotional and physical are all connected.

11. One off, all off. Dial in your zone as if it's an art form. Be an artist!

Powerful trigger words/affirmations

Now that the big picture has come into view, let me give you a few examples of the kind of trigger words you can use to fortify your new attitudes, or replace your current thinking with more productive thoughts. It's better if the trigger words come from you personally, but here are a few sample mantras to help you find and stay in your zone.

1. I'm adapting to my new attitudes well.
2. My focus is to play my style/game.
3. I'm in control of my style.
4. I choose how and when and as it relates to my style.
5. Winning and losing are functions of my style.
6. I can put my ego aside and take the incremental step.
7. Winning is taking the incremental step.
8. I'm my own competition and my goal is to stretch the upper limits of my ability.
9. I'm great at automating my game and incrementally adapting my tactics to my opponent as necessary.
10. My style is so automated, even my adaptations have become automated. I understand conscious thought decreases flow.
11. I'm aware of the mental, physical, and emotional connection, and can dial in my intensity levels with little effort.
12. I feel completely self-liberated, fearless and in the instinctive moment.
13. I can trigger a positive bio-chemical event in my body at will.
14. I'm good at moving my physiology away from my nerves and pressure. I love the battle!
15. My thoughts, emotions, and visual skills are more disciplined which helps my competitive play.
16. My thoughts are present, positive, and relevant to this moment.

17. I love my empowering inner voice when it comes to match play.
18. I am learning from and adapt my style well to my mistakes.
19. My style's improving and I love it.
20. I'm playing with less pressure and enjoying my game much more!

As you progress mentally, you will experience a "shimmy" between your old and new attitudes until the new attitude is actualized. In time, you'll find your new philosophy is more empowering and lifting your game.

The end result is you will be playing with more flow, less worry and greater awareness of how to enter your zone and stay there longer. All in all, a more beautiful expression of yourself on the court!

Steps to peaking at the right time

To peak at the right time or season is more of a science than a random occurrence. "Periodization training" is the name for a time-tested method used to segment training steps and help athletes peak at a designated time.

A periodization program could run from just a few weeks to a full off-season, depending on the situation. I highly recommend you find an experienced coach to tailor an individual program to meet your needs. A sample periodization training program in sequence might be:

1. A constructive rest period phase to mentally, emotionally and physically prepare for the peak season.
2. A conditioning, agility and/or weight training phase.

3. An aerobic or anaerobic training phase.
4. A technical or motor-skill training phase.
5. A strategic or tactical phase.
6. A mental toughness phase.
7. A warm-up competitive play or pre-tournament phase culminating in peaking at a pre-determined season or competition.

A good periodization program gives you time to integrate and improve your game with limited emotional frustration and less chance of injury.

Pre- and post-match evaluation sheet

The post-match evaluation sheet will increase your success fourfold because it moves your focus from the win or the loss (outcome based philosophy) to the process of taking the incremental step (performance based philosophy). Take joy regardless if you win or lose the match in the small incremental successes your making along the way. Use the sheet on page 46 prior to and after matches to chart your progress. Take it to your coach so he or she can help you prioritize your steps.

Conclusion

Now that you've moved into process with better attitudes, tactics and a more powerful inner voice, there are two important questions you should ask yourself after every match:

1. Did I represent myself, my team, my club and the tennis community well, and

2.   Did I give my very best effort?

All in all, think of the book as a launching pad for your tactical A-B-C game plans, your mental toughness philosophies, and ongoing technical and strategic mastery. I hope you've found a few universal truths in this book that you can apply to your everyday life. I wish you a life filled with inspiration and significance well beyond your sport. My greatest hope is that this book helps you find a more beautiful expression of yourself on and off the court!

Please see my additional (quick-fix) books. Each book is uniquely designed to anticipate and address the philosophies, skills, and mindsets necessary for players and coaches to grow and flourish in their favorite tennis disciplines. These books make the perfect gift for all aspiring tennis enthusiasts!

EVALUATION SHEET

Technical incremental steps   Rate 1 - 5

1.
2.
3.

Strategic incremental steps   Rate 1 - 5

1.
2.
3.

Mental/emotional incremental steps   Rate 1 - 5

1.
2.
3.

What adjustments did I make during the match?   Rate 1 – 5

1.
2.
3.

What did I do well?

1.
2.
3.

What areas do I need to improve?

1.
2.
3.

REVIEW: EXPRESSIONS THAT WIN

Strategy

After you've read the "How do I beat any style" sections come back to this section and review what you could also apply to your match play. Then add the incremental steps to your evaluation sheet prior to your next match or practice session to move toward mastery.

1. Consistency – ability to play one more ball back because percentages favor your opponent missing the next shot. Consistency can never be underestimated as one of the greatest weapons in tennis.

2. Control – the ability to play shot combinations and tactics to play your strength and exploit your opponent's weaknesses.

3. Place the serve or return so you can play your favorite shot on the next ball. Where do you have to place the ball in the service box or return serve to a certain area of the court so your opponents' tendency is to play into your strength to begin each point.

4. Play above net level – ability to hit the ball on the rise above net level with a high to low swing path and finish shots or create errors from opponent.

5. Rhythm – The ability to change the composure of your shots such as excessive spin, speed, and height to affect your opponent to timing, make them think and force them into secondary shots.

6. Tempo – ability to consistently dictate the time in-between you and your opponent's shots. Take away your opponents time with an aggressive shot and then

incrementally take more time with each additional shot until you force an error or win the point..

7. Strike zone – ability to place the ball low or high out of your opponent's strike zone.

8. Power – ability to overpower opponents to create forced errors and winners.

9. Court position – ability to hit on the rise from the baseline without running back and play short balls more offensively above net level.

10. Time – ability to take time from opponents on offensive shots and buy time to recover on defensive shots. Time is your most valued commodity in tennis.

11. Pace – ability to change pace to a hard or soft shot to exploit your opponent's preference.

12. Movement – ability to move opponent three steps on each shot to create poor timing, control, power, and receive back balls you can attack.

13. Step up – ability to put opponents on defense, move up into no man's land, split step, evaluate and accelerate to the ball and finish volleys.

14. One up – ability to problem solve and find one thing you better than your opponent and exploit it.

Mental toughness

After you've read the mental toughness section come back to this section and review what you could apply to your match play, then add the incremental steps to your evaluation sheet prior to your next match or practice secession to move toward mastery.

1. Keep a universal perspective that tennis is just a game; humility and grace are the pinnacle of your tennis expression; and there are a lot of people suffering in the word.

2. See winning as improving; understand improving at winning is improving; and develop an insatiable desire to come off the court a better player regardless of the match outcome.

3. Resolutely believe in the strengths of your game. Know that you are yout own competition, with one goal: to to take the incremental step and stretch the upper limits of your ability.

4. Create a bubble around yourself to keep internal and external voices from building irrelevant pressure before your competitions.

5. Analyze your opponents and develop a game plan to exploit their weaknesses.

6. Anticipate the anticpiation of when you need a tactical momentum switch and act decisively.

7. Create and sustain a positive image without showing your opponent any signs of visual weakness or frustration.

8. Keep a positive inner voice and let thoughts that are not present, positive and relevant pass through your mind without attaching to them.

9. Breathe through nerves, reduce heart rate to recover and stop irrelevant thoughts at will, so that you can enter the zone faster and stay there longer.

10. Move your inner physiology to create a biochemical event in your body by more disciplined thinking, feeling,

and visualizing when you're not experiencing a peak performance state of being.

11. Be non-judgmental after mistakes, focus on the present moment, and automate another solution without carrying over past emotions to the next point.

12. See pressure as a challenge not a threat, and create ongoing mindsets that you're really going to enjoy the pressure-filled moments. The ball doesn't know who you are playing or what the score is.

13. Recreate the feelings of your best past performance day and summon up those feelings just prior to big match play moments.

14. Anticipate adversity and respond in a way that allows you to maintain your peak performance state.

15. Enjoy longer gaps of no-mind as you adapt and automate your game, until your adaptations have become automated.

Thank you for reading *Tennis Strategy: How to Beat Any Style Player*. If you enjoyed this book, please consider leaving a review at amazon.com.

Additionally, if you found this guide helpful, please check out my other individualized, quick-fix guides.

Tennis Strategy for Junior Tournament Players
Tennis Strategy for High School Coaches
Singles Strategy: High Percentage Tennis
Doubles Strategy: High Percentage Tennis (Coming Soon)

Made in the USA
San Bernardino, CA
15 October 2016